A BOY IN WARTIME

1939 – 1945

Alan Hill

British Library Cataloguing in Publication Data:

a catalogue record for this publication

is available from the British Library

ISBN 978-1-912052-63-9

Typeset in 12pt Minion Pro at Haddington, Scotland

Printed by West Port Print, St Andrews

Contents

For my children,
Kate and Chris,
and my grandchildren,
Jamie, Milo, Marni and Lara.

Other poetry titles by Alan Hill:

The Green Tide, Rivelin Press, 1975
To Rocamadour, Redbeck Press, 2005
No Biography, HappenStance Press, 2010
Gerontion, HappenStance Press, 2016

Author's Note

During the first Lock-Down I realised two things simultaneously – that 2020 was the 75th. Anniversary year of the end of World War Two, and that I had spoken very little to my children about my memories of that war, and not at all to any of my grandchildren. Perhaps because I was then in my eighty-seventh year, it suddenly seemed important that I should do so while I still could. But my family is widely scattered, and given the pandemic, yarning about the past is no longer an option. What would traditionally have been passed on orally now has to be written.

I began in prose, but my memories weren't having any of that, and I was struggling. The alternative was verse, which seemed odd for such material; and what style of verse? After much experiment I remembered Sir Philip Sidney's line: "Fool," said my Muse to me, "Look in thy heart and write." Good advice. I remembered not just events, but increasingly how I had felt about them, and allowed each memory to determine how it wanted to be written. I think the result is not all that far from someone chatting by a fireside.

Throughout my life, history and literature have been my close companions. On my first visit to Kenilworth Castle, it proved to be what I think is sometimes called a portal; I walked through it and, as I moved round, successive ages came to life for me. I discovered that the past is as real as the present; the only differences are that it is not now, and we don't know it as well as the present, or in the same way. We know it from surviving artefacts, and from written records that people left us. That is why I am recording these few memories of an ordinary child who lived at a very extraordinary time – a few more grains for the ever-growing sandhills of knowledge about our species.

Prologue

"I am speaking to you from the Cabinet Room of 10 Downing Street. This morning the British Ambassador in Berlin handed the German government a note, stating that unless we heard from them – by 11 o'clock – that they were prepared at once to withdraw their troops from Poland, a state of war would exist between us. I have to tell you now that no such undertaking has been received and that, consequently, this country is at war with Germany."

From Prime Minister The Right Honourable Neville Chamberlain's speech to the British people on the B.B.C. Home Service at 11.15 am on Sunday, September 3rd 1939.

I was not yet six years old, but I remember very well being with my parents listening to that speech. I knew from their hushed gravity that this was something of the greatest importance. I remember the defeated sadness of the man's voice, and even now I cannot read those words without feeling a sense of great sadness myself. I think they may have been the saddest words uttered by any British politician during my lifetime. I did not realise it of course, but they were to shape the childhoods of myself and hundreds of thousands of other young children, and so of course, our lives.

Air Raid Precautions ('The Phoney War')

It was a nineteen-thirties "model" school.
The classroom walls that faced to the south
consisted of windows like barn doors
that opened wide for fresh air and sunlight.
Across the playground were garden plots
offering the same, but with exercise
and the satisfaction of watching seeds
grow into vegetables and flowers.
But the only things that grew in his time
were the air raid shelters, an even row
of parallel humps like piglets trying to
suckle from a vanished sow.

The teachers had a good idea.
Each child should bring a tin of sweets
clearly labelled with their names, of course,
saved from their precious sweet rations.
These were to keep the children cheerful
if there should ever be a long air raid.
Soon there was a rehearsal, with the promise
they would be allowed one sweet as a treat.
The tins were opened – a moment of silence –
then forty-three voices raised in dismay.
Every tin was empty; not a sweet to be seen!
They couldn't blame Hitler's Luftwaffe for that.

First Air Raid

His mother struggling to get him dressed.
He struggling to stay asleep.

But the cold night air woke him,
and the searchlight beams criss-crossing the black sky.
Already there were guns firing in the distance.

The air-raid shelter was improvised,
dug by neighbours in a garden –
an angled trench (First World War pattern)
roofed with timber, and soil on top.

They sat in the dark on wooden benches,
their backs to the earth walls.

The gunfire grew louder as planes approached,
local guns in action now,
the noise chaotic
as if all the dogs in the district were barking
at the same time in wild alarm
through huge loudspeakers.

Then bombs howling down,
their pitch falling the lower they fell
like homing missiles seeking them out,
louder and louder, nearer and nearer until
each explosion shook the ground.

He was excited.
It was better than a cowboy film.
Much louder.

A brief lull, then more bombs.
"Hark," he said, "they're getting closer."
An elderly neighbour, Mrs Mason, gave a groan.
"I wish he'd shut up," she said, and Mum hushed him.

Later it grew quiet, but he was still alert.
"What's that noise?" he said. "A sort of rattle."

After a moment Mrs Mason spoke again.
"It's my teeth," she said. "I just can't keep 'em still."

It was getting light when the ALL CLEAR sounded.

Little Pink Clouds

Little pink clouds of smoke
chickenpoxed the dawn sky
after the long air-raids.
Pretty now, they'd already dropped
their metal fragments that had tinkled
and pinged on the stone pavement
as Dad hurried them to the shelter,
ducking under the thunder of shell-bursts.

Those three-point-sevens in Poppet Lane
and the four-point-fives up the main road
had been firing all night.
He could tell them apart.
The three-sevens sounded like
the slamming of double doors –
An echo from the woods his Dad said.
The bigger guns crashed like huge drums.

At six years old he was
steady under fire.
And why not? Those people
who were hurt were the actors;
he was in the audience.

The Balloon

It was Sunday. Dinner-time.
He was standing with his Dad
who was talking to a neighbour at the front gate.

There was a huge BANG
and the sound of breaking glass.
His Dad pushed him down and lay over him.

They waited for more bangs, but all they heard
was men shouting in the field behind the houses
over the road, where the barrage balloon was.

"It's the balloon," Dad said. "It must have exploded."

They went indoors, but the living-room was a mess.
The glass light-shade over the dining-table
had shattered into fragments which were scattered
over the dinner his mother had just brought in.

He'd never seen his mother crying before,
nor his father so gentle and so softly spoken.

Evacuee

Just seven years old and very excited
going on a train to be evacuated

the billeting lady trudged them from house to house
he was the last to be taken the lady at the door
said she didn't know what t'maister would say

he was big now but he'd brought his friend Teddy
he couldn't remember a time without his friend

he was to share a bed with Derek
but Derek wanted to share Teddy

later Derek called down Mam, t'little lad's cryin'

Sunday dinner began with pudding
Yorkshire pudding with pink custard

mostly it seemed he had chips and cocoa
when he went home they said he'd turned yellow

Mr Paget came in sometimes
he wore a cap and kept it on
and dirty white plimsolls with holes at the toes

he'd given his lad a good hiding he said because
he hadn't fought back when another lad hit him

Mr Paget never smiled nor did ’tmaister
once he’d washed ’tmaister’s water bottle with soap
and ’tmaister had shouted
he needed it down’t pit
and it mustn’t be soapy he’d said

from the bedroom window beyond the houses
there was nothing but treetops as far as he could see
he was sure it was Sherwood Forest it must be
he wished he could go there

Dad brought him home just before Christmas
on the way they stopped at a café
that was upstairs over a baker’s shop
but Teddy stayed in the car
their food came on a lift that rumbled
as it was pulled up with a rope
he had sausages mashed potato and swede
still one of his best things ever.

Incendiary Triptych

1 Lost Leader

The hedge at the top of the field
was burning, a long line of fire
with black silhouettes of men moving
in front of the flames like Hell's devils
which he must have seen in a picture somewhere

He knew that his dad was one of them,
air-raid wardens and fire-watchers,
desperately trying to put out
the flames before more enemy planes
could drop their high-explosive bombs on
what was supposed to be their target,
but must have been a navigator's error.

2 Hurray for Duds!

In the cold grey of dawn
after a long air-raid
their neighbout knocked the door.

"There's a hole in your roof," he said.
Dad climbed into the loft, but found
only bits of broken tile.

In the garden though, by a bush,
lay a battered incendiary bomb.
It was a dud that hadn't worked.
"Hurray for duds!" they said.

3 Coventry

The air-raid sirens had wailed as usual,
but there'd been neither planes nor gunfire.
Yet the ALL CLEAR stubbornly refused to sound.

It was in the cold small hours of the morning
when Dad came to their shelter and looked in.
"You should come up and look at this," he said.
They clambered up and looked where he pointed.
Eastward, the sky was just one
huge unearthly orange-coloured glow.

"That's Coventry burning," he said,
"and it's all of eighteen miles away."
That moving, flickering blaze was so intense
it looked as though the sky itself was burning.

Tracer Bullets

It had been a quiet night.
Some anti-aircraft guns had been firing
and they'd heard some bangs that sounded like bombs,
all in the distance though. Nothing very close.
But still the ALL CLEAR hadn't sounded
although nothing seemed to be happening.
They didn't see Dad much during air-raids.
He was a warden and the raids kept him busy,
but tonight he came to the shelter and said
"It's quiet. D'you want to come up for a minute?"

Did he want to! He was up like a shot.
toy tin helmet clamped to his head.
They stood side by side looking up at the sky.
"There it is again. Look at that," Dad said.
There were faint dark red streaks
moving in a line but with spaces between them
like a single thread of red stitching,
seeming to float along one track.
"Tracer bullets," Dad said.

But there was nothing to shoot at,
and he wondered about that.
And he thought the bullets must fall
somewhere, sooner or later.
He wondered about that too.

Unexploded Bomb

The bomb fell in a back garden just up the road. It was where his friend Audrey lived. She was three years older than him; she'd taken him to school when he was five. The bomb had landed just outside their Anderson shelter. Her dad stumbled into the hole when he came out of the shelter. All the people living in the road had to go and stay somewhere else until the bomb was made safe (they hoped).

He decided that even if the war hadn't finished by the time he was grown up, he wouldn't join a Bomb Disposal Unit. First they had to find the bomb; they could see the hole, but they'd no idea how deep it had gone, or if it was tangled up with underground pipes or cables, and until they found it they had no idea what sort of bomb it was, and until they knew that, they didn't know if they could make it safe.

They needed to know why it hadn't exploded. It might have a timing mechanism set to explode later (they used stethoscopes to listen to it). If it was ticking they knew it *would* explode, but not *when.* They needed to find *and remove* the inspection plate to get that information, and to cut the detonator wires (if they could recognise them).

If it wasn't "delayed action" then it was faulty, and they had to steam out the explosive - without jolting or disturbing the bomb in any way. At any stage of these proceedings the bomb *might* explode. These men seemed to stay cheerful. They used to say that if the bomb did explode they wouldn't know anything about it. No, he would not join that unit!

Collateral Damage

When they had to move out
they took the budgie with them.
It's true it was drab and nondescript but
it had a very big personality.
A non-talker, it squawked and chattered
all the more as if to compensate.
Full of *joie de vivre* and huge pizzaz,
as though it was show-biz born and bred
all it needed was an audience
and it would give an amazing display
of acrobatics round its cage
concluding by ringing its bell -
and sometimes by wearing it.

The weather was fine, and it seemed to enjoy
being outside in the open-air,
and that pleased their hosta very well.
The cage was slightly damaged though, and
you couldn't get spares because of the war.
One day they heard an unusual noise,
and went out to find the cage empty.
They never saw the budgie again.
In the terms of frequent wartime announcements
it was "Posted missing. Presumed dead."

Mrs Cowley

He dreaded meeting Mrs Cowley.
She lived in his aunty's village and
her husband had been killed in the war.

He wasn't supposed to know. Well,
not the details, anyway,
but he knew enough to make him

shudder. He'd been reading while
his mother and his aunty talked.
When they spoke softly he tuned in,

something single children learn quickly.
He heard the name, then "... identity disc ..."
then "... they thought a tank ... gone over him ..."

The voices sank below hearing, but
he'd heard enough to piece together,
and he wished he hadn't.

He dreaded meeting Mrs Cowley.
He thought he should say something,
but he didn't know what.

Picture Post

He was visiting Grandma's with his mother.
Grandma and Grandad had been bombed out
and now they were living in temporary lodgings.
In the confusion their house had been looted;
thieves, presumably looking for money,
had taken papers, photographs, documents;
of little value, but their loss distressing..

Mum and Grandma had things to discuss
and needed to go in the other room,
so he was invited to read a magazine.
He found ***Picture Post*** and felt relieved. It was
big on pictures and you didn't have to read
the serious print if you didn't want to.

This number was about the Japanese
occupation of China, and ill-treatment
of Chinese civilians. The brutality
shocked him deeply. A picture he couldn't get
out of his mind was of two prisoners
awaiting execution. They were bound
to posts with barbed wire, sweating with fear,

while two Jap soldiers with fixed bayonets
stood by in the foreground, grinning hugely.

What he read there disturbed him even more –
children often don't interrogate text
with care – and it seemed to him that these men's
heads had been sawn off with bayonets.
Calmly his older self would try to reason that
bayonets are seldom edged weapons, and
in any case the beheading was
probably *post mortem*, for grim display
to "encourage" other civilians to toe
a particular Japanese line.

Whatever the truth, he found a box
in his head where he dropped the whole article
and slammed down the lid. If he had known about
radio-active isotopes he would have felt
that he had one locked in a box in his head.

BBC News

He followed the war with interest, and
listened to news bulletins carefully.
One day he heard that Japanese soldiers
had raked European woman prisoners.
He was astonished. He couldn't think why
they would do such a thing, or indeed how.
He knew what a rake was; had often used one
himself in the garden. He guessed their
purpose was to cause disfigurement,
and thought it was very cruel.
He asked his mother about it,
but she seemed no wiser than he was.
It was a mystery.

Unequal Combat

Mid-afternoon.
He was with his mother who was visiting a friend.
In fact he was in the garden, mucking about.
He was bored.
But boredom outside was liberty compared with
boredom indoors, listening to conversation.

Then he heard an aeroplane's engines.
He thought it sounded like a German bomber.
But that wasn't possible, not in daylight.
And besides, the sirens hadn't sounded.
He knew there was no way a German plane
could fly the hundred miles from the East Coast
in broad daylight without being challenged
and shot down.

He saw it then. There was no doubt.
It was a Heinkel bomber. He was sure.
He was an avid and regular reader
of the aircraft-recognition manuals
his father brought home.

And then he heard a Spitfire's engine,
a sound he knew only too well because
he lived under the flight-path of new Spitfires
that were tested every day from
the nearby factory where they were made.
They flew so low he waved to the pilots.

It was coming up fast, and it wasn't a test-flight;
he could hear its machine-guns, tat-a-tat tat-a-tat,
and then the rough grunts of its cannons, too.

Suddenly hands seized him by the shoulders,
whirled him round and hustled him indoors.
"Mum! OH MUM" and he rushed to the window
but was instantly whisked away from there too.

"Don't be so silly......stray bullets.
You could be ***KILLED!"***
"But MUM, I'm ***MISSING IT***"
"Enough," she said. And that was that.

Blackpool Sands

Blackpool sands were golden, smooth and wide,
and cleansed twice daily by the Irish tide;
a great place for trippers if it wasn't raining,
and even when it was, for young airmen's training –
running, exercises and basic skill
in military movement and weapons drill.
He thrilled to watch their yelling bayonet practice,
the good old-fashioned way to beat the Axis.*
Though as he watched he saw some IFs and BUTs.
Could *he* stab Japs or Germans in the guts?
He'd thought a bayonet charge a path to glory,
but was the real thing a different story?
And what if they should scream, or beg for mercy . . . ?

*The Axis Powers – Germany, Italy and Japan, also with Hungary, Romania, Slovakia & Bulgaria.

Dripping on Toast

At weekends they always had a Sunday roast
which fed them a second time, cold, on Mondays.
They kept the dripping that ran from the meat
because so many kinds of food were scarce that
they needed all the nutrition they could get.
It tasted especially good in winter
spread on toast made at an open coal fire
by spearing it on a long toasting-fork
until it was crisped to a rich golden-brown.
The savoury dripping ran into the toast
but when you crunched it, out it ran again
into your mouth like liquid roast beef or roast pork.
And Oh the brown jelly that was under the fat!
It just didn't get any better than that.

Sunday Afternoon

Winter. Sunday afternoon. Gathering dusk.
They were all sitting by the fire, reading.
The light was changing; not exactly getting dimmer,
but – changing colour? Yes, changing colour.
There was something strange about it; eerie,
as though something unknown were about to happen.

Restless now, he went to the window and looked out.
A strong red glow. Sunset? No. Wrong position.
Close to the glass now he looked upward,
but couldn't understand what he saw -
a huge mass of orange fire, as if
the blazing sun were falling to the earth.
"Dad! Dad, quick!" And Dad came very quickly.
"Oh my God," he said, "it's the barrage balloon.
And he rushed out to the Wardens' Post
to raise the alarm.

It missed the houses,
but all that evening they could hear
the homely *Heave-Ho*-ing
of the aircraftmen hauling
their cable home.

Henry V

1944 > 1599 > 1415

Nineteen-forty-four. Laurence Olivier
rang all the tills of all the cinemas
of Britain with his film adaptation
of William Shakespeare's *Henry The Fifth*.
He rode the British patriotic wave
as surely as he rode his destrier
to lead his British troops to Agincourt –
yes, British. Shakespeare makes a point of it.

Each with the price of a seat in his pocket,
together with Dave, his partner in crime and
boon companion in many adventures,
he set off to town one Saturday afternoon
to the West End Cinema, to take a trip
to fourteen-fifteen through fifteen-ninety-nine.

From the first track-in to the final tableau
they watched spellbound, and as the curtains closed,
with scarce a word they ducked between the seats
and stayed there as the cinema re-filled,
resumed their seats, and watched the film again,
utterly transported in time and space,
their life-paths chosen, though they didn't know.

Troop Trains

The railway cutting at the bottom of
his aunty's garden was always his refuge
when there was nothing particular to do.
It was August again, and with his mother
he was on holiday at his aunty's house.
D-Day was only two months ago and
there was still bitter fighting in Normandy.
There were restrictions on where you could travel
so the railway cutting got to know him well.

There were trains full of soldiers every day.
He knew they were returning from France because
many were wounded, heavily bandaged,
some still bleeding into their bandages.
He was surprised to see no nurses.
They were Americans, but not cheerful.
He waved at first but very few waved back.
Most just stared, as though they didn't see him,
or anything in particular.

He'd seen photographs of men who looked like that –
soldiers in the trenches in the First World War,
their eyes without interest or hope.

Shell Bay

On the chain ferry, Sandbanks to Studland,
the hatch to the engine-room was open.
He heard the hiss of the piston's exhaust,
and watched the crankshaft's slow revolutions
hauling the ship on its great iron chains.

Once off the ship, they walked by the water
to Shell Bay to eat their picnic, which Mum
used to do as a child, she told him.
Only the lapping of little wavelets
broke the profound peace of the empty beach.
Apart from the distant barbed wire at
their backs, the war might never have been.

Mum had a book and wanted to read,
but beachcombing was more to his liking.
He'd never seen so many shells in one place.
Their sheer quantity astonished him,
and their variety stoked his curiosity.
In some spots they were clustered into heaps,
and clattered like shale as he scuffed among them –
cockle shells, scallop shells, whelks and winkles,
razor-shells, oyster shells, barnacles, limpets,
and shells he'd never seen before, names unknown –
yet another new one every few minutes.

At high-water mark he reached the barbed wire
where, on his belly, he wriggled underneath
to glean some undisturbed super-specimens.
When his mother called him for sandwiches
he returned in triumph, mission complete.

They took the shorter route back to the ferry
along the edge of the barbed wire.
It was only then they saw the notices
posted at intervals along the wire.
The notices said: DANGER MINES.

Snowballs

It was August, but there were Snowballs in town –
in shiny white helmets and snappy white gaiters.
They were American Military Police.
He thought it was an odd name to give them,
but he saw the point, and he thought it made
an interesting contrast to the British 'Red Caps".
He'd seen them as sentries standing outside
the American Headquarters building,
a handsome old house they'd taken over
right in the centre of the old town.

But he felt uncertain about their function.
True, the Snowballs didn't carry guns, but
they carried heavy truncheons with leather thongs,
which they swung about with nonchalant abandon –
an unnecessary show of brute force, he felt.
Everyone knew the British police carried batons,
but discreetly, out of sight, in special pockets.
He felt that swinging those long truncheons
put the Snowballs somewhere between
real-life thugs and The Keystone Cops.

Entr'acte

The war in Europe was over.
The school's evacuated section had returned.
Tradition was being re-asserted.

Last day of term in warm July.
After the longed-for final dismissal
(masters and prefects mysteriously missing)
they marched through the corridors, arms linked, chanting
No more Latin, no more Greek,
No more flipping prefects' cheek!
No more Latin, no more French,
No more sitting on the old school bench!

So they were released into living again,
into that long idyllic dream of summer.
Into freedom, leisure, and time simply to be.

Newsreels

The up-beat commentator's voice
bounced out the bold syllables
in approved style,
narrating how the Allied forces
were taking over the administration
of broken Germany and its ruins.
But when it came to the liberation
of the concentration camps,
that *bonhomie*
failed.

Longer silences lapsed between shots.
Words would not go there.
What they were watching
was beyond understanding or imagination;
horror unrelated to anything known.
One shot he didn't recognise at first –
the nature of the rubbish
some soldiers were moving –
swinging what looked like
long narrow bundles of limp cloth
from a pile, on to a lorry.
Then he realised they were human bodies;
had once been people.

Chewing-gum

He was back in one of his favourite places,
the Southern Railway main-line track
that ran at the bottom of his aunty's garden.
Summer holidays on the south coast again,
but this time alone; Mum was coming later.
Trainspotting was his default activity,
so here he was, bright and early, hoping for
a King Arthur Class (four-six-o) to start the day.
Later there'd be the backwater to explore –
hopping the tussocks among the mudflats
and scrambling through the carcasses of old beached boats.

A whistle from the right-hand side – train coming!
The wire fence beside him jangled – André arrived –
the boy from next door with the French mother.
The train was carrying American soldiers;
André instantly ducked through the wires –
"Got any gum Chum?" he yelled at each carriage.
A languid arm tossed something through a window.
Once the train passed, André went down the slope,
eyes fixed, like a terrier going for a ball.
Then he clambered back with a small packet,
tearing it open as he came. "D'you want a piece?"
he said, "It's strawberry." They tried it in silence.
"D'you always get gum?" he asked. "Mostly," André said.

The August sun was already burning
so it seemed a good idea to light a fire.
André's garden was a victim of the war.
A hidden trellis sagged under a vast
rambler rose. "We'll prune that," André said.
Rose cuttings, they found, burn very fiercely
in an old oil-drum with a strong draught.
They worked till sweat and grime ran down their faces,
then sat on old bricks to drink lemonade,
and fell into quiet companionable chat.

But then André groaned. "Here's Margie," he said.
She came without ceremony through the garden,
tall and thin, brown with sunburn, her sharp face
framed by a straggle of greasy black ringlets.
"What you doin'?" she said. André glared.
"We're standin' on our heads ringin' handbells," he said.
"There's no call to be rude," she said, with prim care.
"All right. Find some bricks and sit down then," he said.
"You want some chewing-gum?" She tried it with interest.
"Oh, it's strawberry." she said. "Where you get it?"
"American soldiers; off the trains," he said.

She leapt to her feet as though she'd been stung,
spat out the gum and went on spitting as if it were poison.
Horrified, André said "What you do that for?"
"Ugh! Those American soldiers are filthy!"
she said, getting rid of any slight remainder.
"What d'you mean?" he said, still bewildered.
She needed no coaxing but launched straight into
a series of dreadful revelations –
the source being her "friend, who's sixteen," she said,
alleging quite bizarre sexual habits
embracing much, he was almost certain,
that was anatomically impossible.
It seemed that many American soldiers
were off their heads – or that Margie was; but
he suspected that she was the victim
of someone's fevered imagination.
He didn't believe that a girl of her age
would know enough even to invent such stories.
She ended her shocking exposée of
American military manhood by
declaring she'd "never go out with one!"
Lacking tact he asked her "How old are you?"
Glancing back sharply she said "How old are you?"
In his world fencing was done with swords, not words.
"Eleven," he said. "I'm twelve," she said very quickly.
"No you're . . ." André started . . . "I'm twelve!" she snapped

"There's a condom in the air-raid shelter," she said.
It's not the word she used, but it's what she meant.
Their blank faces called for information,
which she was graciously pleased to supply.
She offered to show them, taking silence for assent.
Privately he was sure this would prove to be
the somebody-must-have-moved-it routine,
and followed in sceptical confidence.
But she emerged with a limp bedraggled thing
waving it triumphantly over her head.
The boys fell back with cries of disgust,
then André said quietly,
with matter-of-fact conviction,
"You're a dirty cow, Margie."
Her only response was a harsh laugh.

Ice Cream

The horrors of two atomic explosions
persuaded the Japanese to surrender.
It was August, and finally the whole of
the Second World War was over.
But the Pacific was a long way away
and besides, there were people who worried that
the atom bomb caused more problems than it solved.

But where he was, these troubles were eclipsed
by the most exciting news he could remember.
The little general shop just over the road was
selling ICE CREAM! He could dimly remember it
from being at the seaside before the war
and always dropping his ice-cream cornet before
he could finish it, and his stricken grief.

This time it was very different –
Lyon's Dairy Maid in neat little cylinders
designed to fit snugly on top of the cone.
He'd grown very deft now and lost not a drop.
And he found too that bonfires and fireworks
had their own magical exhilarations, but
lacked that deep inner satisfaction of ice cream.

Crabbing

It was bright and sunny
and a brisk wind was pushing the tide in.
The crabs were lively, eager to feed,
throwing themselves on the bacon rinds
the boys had managed to scrounge.

The crabs were determined, clinging to the bait
even as it was rising up from the water,
suspecting no danger till they touched concrete,
when they would suddenly scuttle for safety,
always in the right direction and always
running recklessly over the edge.
to drop down and splash back into the water.

Already the catch was twenty-three – best ever –
when André pulled up number twenty-four.
Huge and very obstinate, it still hung
on to the bait, ignoring the concrete.
André picked it up to get a closer look,
holding the carapace well behind the claws.
It was a monster, and they gazed at it with pride.

Just then Margie arrived. "What you doin'?" she said.
"Crabbin," André said. "We've got twenty-four,
and we've just caught this monster. Look."
She shrieked and recoiled. "He won't hurt you,"

André said, “Watch.” He set it down on the concrete,
and as expected, it scuttled back towards the water.
It wasn’t going her way at all, but
she moved with feral speed and smashed
her shoe down with such force on it
that bits of crab were scattered about.

He thought André was going to attack her.
She thought so too and began to back away.
“You cow!” he shouted. “You rotten cow!
“What you do that for? He wasn’t hurtin’ you.”
Snarling insults, she retreated, and fled.

“She always ruins everythin’,” André said,
as they scuffed the monster’s remains
back into the water.

Farewell to Wartime

It was a bright sunny morning
when he walked with his mother
along the Esplanade to the station.
His uncle, gassed in the First World War,
gallantly carried his mother's case.
A fresh south-westerly breeze
plucked up the water into little wavelets
that sparkled in the sunlight.

Their train rapidly gathered speed
under the footbridge and into the cutting,
past his aunt's garden where a boy was waiting
on the wire fence, with both arms waving.
But the rails began coiling into the bend
and his last sight of André was abruptly lost.

Epilogue

Troy

Sometimes I remember that little wood
where four bombs fell and blew out craters like
great pudding-basins in the black leaf mould.

Up in one corner was the wooden stile
that led to the cornfield and the path home;
downhill opposite, the gate to the lane,
the small green, the cottages and the pump;
and the right-hand fork to Poppet Lane
where the anti-aircraft battery waited
to shatter calm nights of dangerous moonlight
defending us with its thunderous lightning.

But no trace of any of that remains,
where once I explored life as a young boy.
All built on. Buried now, like a layer of old Troy.